Braided

poems by

Leslie Shiel

Finishing Line Press
Georgetown, Kentucky

Braided

Copyright © 2017 by Leslie Shiel
ISBN 978-1-63534-126-3 First Edition
All rights reserved under International and Pan-American Copyright Conventions.
No part of this book may be reproduced in any manner whatsoever without written permission from the publisher, except in the case of brief quotations embodied in critical articles and reviews.

ACKNOWLEDGMENTS

Kestrel: "Grotto"
New Virginia Review: "The Laying On of Hands"
New Zoo Poetry Review: "Knots"
Sow's Ear Poetry Review: "White Shorts under Our Skirts"
The Comstock Review: "Constancy"
The 4x4 Newport Review: "POW"
The Southern Review: "New Year's Eve A.A. Dance"
The Sun: "Euphemism"

Publisher: Leah Maines

Editor: Christen Kincaid

Cover Art: *Hair Work*, A. Stoeber, engraver; A. Beillet, printer; P. Florentin, artist. The New York Public Library Digital Collections

Author Photo: Briget Ganske

Cover Design: M.A. Keller

Printed in the USA on acid-free paper.
Order online: www.finishinglinepress.com
   also available on amazon.com

> Author inquiries and mail orders:
> Finishing Line Press
> P. O. Box 1626
> Georgetown, Kentucky 40324
> U.S.A.

Table of Contents

Grotto 1

Intercession 4

White Shorts under Our Skirts 5

The Laying On of Hands 6

Euphemism 8

New Year's Eve A.A. Dance 9

POW 11

Real World 12

On the Bench 14

Sitting with My Father, 81, after a Stroke 16

Keeping Track 17

Braided 18

Conception 21

Constancy 23

Knots 24

*for the girls still running—wildly—
through the grotto*

The tearing of the veil is so that we may see humanity—including our own humanity—as well as God.

—Rowan Williams
Ponder These Things: Praying with Icons of the Virgin

Grotto

Called by a bell
to where Polish monks
flow through strong
doorways, their hands
fingering long ropes
at their sides, Camille and I

insert fliers, dipping
sponges into cups
of water, sealing
envelopes to earn
our scout badge. Shy,
pre-teen, we wait,

giggling at language
we don't understand, until,
released, we run
wild under grapevines
leading to the statue Saint
Bernadette. The dark-haired

Jennifer Jones played
the saint in the movie.
When the old nun asked
if she suffered, Bernadette
pulled up her skirt, exposing
the bones of a knee wrenched

out of its socket.
At her feet, we kneel,
whispering quick prayers,
afraid we'll have a sudden
vision, see it come alive
or drop real tears. We

don't stay too long,
knowing a saint's dilemma:
whether or not to tell
our parents, risk being thrown
out of their prison
into the world's

boiling oil, not yet
whole. Before the statue,
we struggle to stand,
our own legs banging
against folding chairs
set up for Sunday Mass.

*

In a studio in Muncie,
ten years after following
Camille through the grotto,
I hear church bells,
and in my fear (or love)
consider them

holy: a sign. I call
my fiancé and ask him
to meet me at the all-night diner.
In the rocky parking lot,
he holds me, whispering,
It's only fear. But I try

entering the convent anyway,
the recruiter asking me, *Why?*
I say, *Solitude*—not the answer
she looks for: passion for the unseen
Lord. I don't confess
the beloved at my stairs,

still calling, the real
resonance, the resilient
flame. Now, divorced,
trying to re-think my life again,
I remember the grotto,
how, chanting, we'd kneel

before icons, lighting
candles for the child Christ,
his fingers pointing to stars
trapped in damp ceilings.
Alone, I climb the stairs
to the largest chapel,

where I can't find Camille
(who took the veil)
and am afraid she'll jump out
behind me, screaming. There
the Polish Madonna hangs
scorched, saved once from fire.

Intercession

Choir breaks up the day
the directors clash

and she ushers him out with a slap
louder than wedding bells

they'll never hear. Abandoned
in the basement church, burning

for their teenage romance,
we crawl up the communion aisle

to kiss the virgin's plastic feet.
Annmarie wails, *She's his for keeps.*

White Shorts under Our Skirts

Down dark stairs we march
weekly into the cafeteria for gym, turn right,
line up along the brown tiles, stare up at gold
curtains, wait to answer *here* when our names
are called. The teacher loves girls—
president's council stripes on their shorts—
with legs like my brothers'.

*

Jeanine twists a wire into a spiral,
sticks it up her skirt, and calls it a penis.
I don't laugh. Toes to the line,
arms stiff, I look straight ahead.
Do I lie—*I forgot*—or own up,
feeling the stain spread
as the teacher barks, *Why
haven't you dropped your skirt?*

*

I will fall on another girl's back
who will scream, *I'm smashed, I'm hurt.*
But first, the order to acrobat
in front of the class. I will listen for the whistle
signaling my turn to aim, to run, to hook
my arms under her waist and swing into a headstand.
I will back up. I will close my eyes and pray—
like at a railroad crossing—whispering, *Our Father.*

The Laying On of Hands
    —for Karen Fitzpatrick

The sun falls
too bright through hospital windows.
The smiles drop from our faces.
Acting happy
for your husband and mother
had once been our joke.
You'd fume when they'd leave
and I'd listen. Only now,
you can't talk. To answer questions,
you blink *no*.

        *

Zechariah enters the temple
at the hour of incense. The angel
appears on his right, startling him
into silence, blinding him with words
of gladness and joy, commanding him,
Don't be afraid—
but Zechariah, troubled
into silence of a different kind,
is unable to speak—until the child is born.

        *

Without a knock,
a man in a collar, his
smile too wide,
enters the room,
puts down his bag,
gets out a bible,
which he spreads on your stomach
as if you're a table—
solid, inert.

Eyes open wide, you blink
no—but he prays
over you anyway,
breathing loudly in your face,
asking God for all the things he thinks

you want. Your words
catch in your cancered
throat, noisy
as the wings of the angel.

*

Don't be afraid, the angel ordered
Zechariah, and I watch
the minister lean over you, no
voice in the wilderness, my own
voice caught, until
he removes the book,
then leaning lower, lays his hands
on your chest, fingering
the place your breast used to be.
The laying on of hands—
he whispers, subtly acknowledging
your startled look
                              calling me
back to other times you've warned intruders
with a flash of your arms now paralyzed
at your side, and suddenly I stand
before the angel and Zechariah,
mercifully unable
not to shout—

Euphemism

Like the time I was in fourth grade and my hair
reached all the way down to my butt and my mother
said, "let's get a trim" and my cousin Kathy cut
my hair all the way up to my chin and when my
friend Carol laughed at my "cut" I said it was a
"trim" and she shut up.

Like the time my goldfish Spot died and when I got
home from school and saw his bowl empty my mother sat
me down and said a poor boy had come to the door
and he had no friends or pets so she gave him my fish
because she knew I "wouldn't mind" and when I
rode over to Carol's and she asked what was wrong
I said, "a poor boy has taken my fish" and she was quiet.

New Year's Eve A.A. Dance

This I must admit to you:
when you put on your dress
clothes, I stood in the hall
and recognized the sober
appearance of a suit that counted
twenty years ago, a slip

of the past you tried to slip
past me. I recognized you
and tried not to count
it against you. My own dress,
blue and sober,
stuck to my hose in the hall

at the dance, where you hauled
me to celebrate a year without slips.
*Just a bunch of sober
drunks*, you
said, loosening the dress
tie, frayed as your countenance

as you counted
couples passing us in the hall.
A woman you knew swirled her dress,
then slipped
you a smile. You
stared at her soberly,

and I thought, *She's sober,
like me, but alone. Whom did she count
on to stay by her side*? You
touched my arm, but we were stuck in the hall.
How does anyone manage to slip
away? You clung to me through my dress.

Earlier, undressed
before you, I was sober
with fear I might slip
and not count
in the long haul
between my recovery or you.

Don't dress me in costumes you counted on.
Sober, I will back down the hall,
then slip out the door without you.

POW

    —for Al Bianucci

Uncle, the task you give me
the last time I see you
is still a seed. *Tell them,*
you say, impatient with
breathing, *we were cold,
dirty, always hungry.*

No one else wants to hear
how once, the guard,
seeing you stop
to carry someone stumbling,
swung the butt of his rifle
into your back
until you dropped.

Sun blinds my eyes
inside this sick room.
I am this story; make me
humble. Bring me up
from my knees
in the telling.

Real World

Just after my father agreed
to never again introduce me as his
*girlfriend, young chick,
wife*, we went for breakfast,
where he said, *my
daughter* to a hostess who asked,
Does she have a name? The air

cleared now
for something other than a fight,
my father told me the story
of his best friend getting off at some port
and never returning, then, how
difficult those first few months
were in college, back from the navy, 1953,
*having seen what we saw
and still . . .* And now, my

student—just back from Iraq—
standing in front of me, fighting
my strict attendance policy, saying,
It's such a small thing . . .
My father told each of his children,
*You're my best
friend,* then, *This is our secret . . .*
In the clanging

student lounge, coins
in machines, the microwave's hum, popcorn
hitting the air-
tight bags moments
after our explosive
first class, the student—this veteran
soldier—shrugs, flips
his folder from hand to hand,
and holding my stare, backs down.

On the Bench
>*Deliver me speedily . . .*
>*Pull me out of the net*
>*that they have laid privily for me.*
>   —*Psalm 31*

    1.

On a scale of one to ten, my father asks,
where do you stand on marriage?
Has something I've done kept you from it?

We sit on a bench at the Pottery
while my boyfriend and mother shop.
Earlier, over the phone, my brother told me,
*He's so afraid you'll go to hell that he's seen
the priest about his 'daughter's shacking up.'*

    2.

In the dentist's office, there for re-alignment,
my father reads the psalm before handing over
his dentures and *hiding out* at home for 24 hours,
reading Billy Graham. *I like him, do you?*
He visited O.J. in prison and told him to read this

psalm which I'd read years earlier, trying to think
like my friend who'd painted an illuminated
text of a two-headed woman, earless,
in bright purples and greens, demanding God-
like-a-tree-that-sways, *Bow down thy ear to me.*

3.

The priest assured my father that his daughter's
sin is not on him. *The big concern,*

my father says to me now, on the bench,
leaning in, repeating the priest's words

while shoppers swirl around us, *is whether
there is a seed—my father whispers, planting—*

of doubt, guilt that will grow and eat her alive.

Sitting with My Father, 81, after a Stroke

In the photo of my baptism
is my father. His crew cut. No smile
like the one of his wedding. His white shirt's
thin grey plaid I look for every time
I pass through the men's aisle, brushing
my hand against sleeves that are not it.
In my hand now, this triptych: the priest
of the Conception (Immaculate), the god-
father named for a wolf, and, jarred
and ill-at-ease with the weight of me—
we weren't ready—my father—*too soon.*

Keeping Track
> *And he was in the wilderness forty days . . .*
> —Mark 1:12-13

Last night, reading one woman's memory of the Holocaust,
I was grateful for the cat on my lap.

You should see my bathroom: animal prints,
a merman mask, a towel rack carved like a dog.

I'm so tired of criticism. I want to be more
of a naturalist, meet wild angels.

I saw ducks with their butts in the air, I tell my class.
A walk a day for 300 days: my answer for how to get poetry back.

I am like a pregnant bear, but not
knowing when to wake and give birth.

Braided

No babydoll's plastic
   curves in my
mother's laundry room—

but a knotted
   limp sock monkey
hung from a hook,

its bright red mouth
   always open. I tried
to thrust off the real

monkey tangled
   in my adolescent hair
on a zoo vacation

in the Ozarks. The trainer—
   I see in the polaroid—
touches my back. My hair

braided, I was
   pretty for the last
time. Years after, bent

over a table, the palm reader's
   long hair draped
my arm. She named me

Monkey—symbol
   of play and surprise. Later,
a friend—now lost to me—

reading a Chinese zodiac
   placemat, corrected me:
Rooster—harsh singer,

teller of truths.
   But no one,
she filled in, herself,

can get past your knots.
   Now, crippled
in meditation, I'm unable

to open. Monkey
   Doll on my pillow says *yes—*
and *no—*then shows me

again the child
   caught in my truck's lights
at the Navajo reservation:

a girl in the middle
   of the road, rocking
her monkey doll. *She can't*

be real. I brake and stall
   until I see—sacramental,
iconic in the chapel

of imagination—Chagall's
   The Rooster: a woman
riding the rooster's back,

her cheek against his head,
　　arms hugging its neck.
I get out of the truck,

listening to the voices
　　of our bodies—dare I
call them *radiant*?—ready

now to walk the girl
　　safely off that road,
her only witness.

Conception

This umbrella from the east
coast, one spoke already broken, won't hold
off a Chicago storm. Three blocks away
from the Art Institute, I swear, shiver,
and duck under an awning, out of thunder,
more entertaining to passing

motorists than the sax player next to me passing
breathy notes to say *I'm here*. The east
is far away. Later, in the museum, thunder
sounds behind Chagall's *America*—windows holding
dancers, candlesticks, birds (in *Liberty*) shivering
in the dark. I've found my way

back to this favorite place, weigh-
station, crossroad, my old life passing
away while a child's new life shivers
around my body's edges. East,
in Virginia, her father waits to hold
the story that says *Yes, let her come*. "Thunder":

same root as "astonishment." Her thundering
heartbeat, her voice, later amplified. The way
to the next gallery clear, I hold
the weather in my hair. Passing
into Hindu art, I stop. *Back east
is still*, my husband wrote, his shivering

hope, a letter in my backpack. *Shiva holds
a rattle*, I read under the sculpture, *to make his own*—thunder
interrupts, prophetic—*rhythms*. In the east,

my next life can't keep quiet. I'm weighed—
alone here—by thoughts of this midwestern home's passing.
Shiva creates as well as—"hold

that," I jot in my book ("hold
me," I think)—*destroys*. Shivering,
I love—and shudder at—the story I pass
through next: Shiva's wife, thundering
with fear, creates a child (alone), a way
of protection. Jealous of her easy

hold, Shiva beheads that son, but thunder
shivers six *more* lives into six blades of grass. New ways
of passing my breath take root in the east.

Constancy
   —*chalk drawing, Dana Littlepage Smith*

My old friend's work on turquoise paper hangs
on my office wall. A stick figure holds hands
with a child behind a parade of three gold ants,
unflinching in their walk. Her muscled arms are purple
lined in black. Tipping a wine glass, a third figure
sways on a whale's back, while inside, Jonah's excuses
break into stars, fish, tears, flame: his story's
newly unraveling long marks of orange—a trumpet's
labored stutter interrupting safer shapes and colors.

Knots
        —for my grandmother, Elvira Zeni Comandella

She takes my tangled necklaces on-
    to her lap and with a straight pin
        works the knots,
then places gold on lilac towels by dishes
    damp on the counter. Her beads,
        clear glass,
the tarnished cross well-worn, now hang on my
    blue nail. Her missal, full
        and black, recedes
to backs of shelves, instead of daily turned
    in shaking hands. The holy
        cards inside
are still. Oh how those saints were prayed to,
    the corners bent and frayed. What words
        did she—
still young—use to speak her grief? Which saint
    spoke back about the son
        who died? Sixteen.
He dove and broke his neck. I'm pregnant, afraid,
    and dreaming her,
        another woman's voice
on death, and birth. *Go on*, she says, *be strong*.
    The saints stay put
        in pictures in her book.
Instead, she comes alone, untangles fears
    that no one else can see,
        then lays them out.

Additional Acknowledgments

Braided is the second chapbook of a trilogy that started with *Self-Portrait as a New Name,* published by Finishing Line Press in 2015. Thank you, again, to the friends and poets acknowledged in the first book, many of whom still support the living and the work. (Maggi Tinsley and John Heroy, I meant to include you there.) Thanks, in particular this time, to early teachers—Mrs. Patricia Hyland (who introduced me to the Hebrew Prophets), Sr. Elaine, Sr. Dorthea (who introduced me to Whitman's poems), Barbara Mayer, Fr. Jim Bates, Dr. Charlie Payne, Dr. Virginia Grabill.

Catherine MacDonald, Tara Bray, Kathy Davis, and Margaret Gibson had a special hand in particular poems for *Braided.* Dana Littlepage Smith's and Steve Scafidi's presence as working poets is instrumental. Claudia Emerson's influence reverberates. Dave Smith continues to teach me.

Thank you to Charlie Martin, Joan Cantwell, and Mike Carson, ongoing oldest friends; and to my mother, Gloria Shiel. I thank Carole Weinstein for encouragement, support, and unfolding conversation about poems and poets. Special thanks to Elizabeth Cooper for constant friendship and support, and for opening the door to a year of writing through the 2016–17 Elizabeth Stanley Cooper Fellowship.

And for the various "grottos"—the Carmelite Monastery in Munster, Indiana; the St. Francis of Assisi Newman Center in Muncie, Indiana; New Harmony, Indiana; the Virginia Center for the Creative Arts; Richmond Friends Meeting; the Richmond Hill Retreat Center; and the fire-lit log cabin of Sam and Susan Cook—I am grateful.

I am deeply appreciative of Michael Keller's skill in poetry, editing, design, and technology. And for daily support, kindness, challenge, humor, and tenderness, I thank both him and Jordan Keller.

Leslie Shiel is the 2016–17 recipient of the Elizabeth Stanley Cooper Fellowship, and her first chapbook, *Self-Portrait as a New Name*, was published by Finishing Line Press in 2015. She teaches at Virginia Commonwealth University, where she received the College of Humanities and Sciences 2014 Distinguished Adjunct Award, and at the Visual Arts Center of Richmond, where she received the 2014 Master Teacher Award. Her poems have been published in *Crab Orchard Review, The Southern Review, Poetry International, The Sun, Nimrod, The Comstock Review, Sow's Ear Poetry Review, Christianity and Literature*, and other journals. She has been the recipient of an Individual Artist Grant from the Virginia Commission for the Arts and has been a resident at the Virginia Center for the Creative Arts. She lives with her husband and daughter in Richmond, Virginia.

www.ingramcontent.com/pod-product-compliance
Lightning Source LLC
LaVergne TN
LVHW041510070426
835507LV00012B/1475